cupcakes

cupcakes

Susannah Blake

photography by Martin Brigdale

RYLAND
PETERS
& SMALL

LONDON NEW YORK

Acknowledgements
For Fred, Eleanor, and little Tomski.

Senior Designer Steve Painter
Commissioning Editor Julia Charles
Editor Rachel Lawrence
Production Gemma Moules
Art Director Anne-Marie Bulat
Publishing Director Alison Starling

Food Stylist Linda Tubby
Prop Stylist Helen Trent
Indexer Hilary Bird

Notes
• All spoon measurements are level, unless otherwise specified.
• All eggs are medium, unless otherwise specified. Uncooked or partly cooked eggs should not be served to the very young, the very old, those with compromised immune systems, or to pregnant women.

Library of Congress Cataloging-in-Publication Data

Blake, Susannah.
  Cupcakes / Susannah Blake ; photography by Martin Brigdale.
    p. cm.
  Includes index.
  ISBN-13: 978-1-84597-379-7
  1. Cake. I. Title.
  TX771.B564 2007
  641.8'653--dc22

2006027134

ISBN-10: 1 84597 379 8
ISBN-13: 978 1 84597 379 7

Printed and bound in China.

First published in the USA in 2007 by Ryland Peters & Small, Inc.
519 Broadway, 5th Floor
New York NY 10012
www.rylandpeters.com

10 9 8 7 6 5 4 3 2

Text © Susannah Blake 2007
Design and photographs
© Ryland Peters & Small 2007

contents

making cupcakes

So utterly cute that no grown adult can resist, cupcakes baked in pretty paper liners are the ultimate in feel-good confectionery. Whether decorated in pretty pastels with dainty sugar flowers or swirled with an indulgently rich, dark chocolate frosting, a plateful of cupcakes is sure to lift your spirits and bring a smile to your face.

You can eat them pretty much any time—mid-morning with a cup of coffee, with a cup of tea at 4 o'clock, or after dinner instead of dessert. They're also great tucked into a lunchbox or in the middle of the night as a cure for those raging midnight munchies. Cupcakes make the perfect gift, too—nestled in a pretty box or basket for a special occasion, or simply taken on a plate to offer as a hostess gift.

The simplest cupcake mixture is made with an equal weight of butter, sugar, eggs, and flour, beaten to a smooth, creamy consistency with a splash of milk, then spooned into muffin cups and baked until risen and golden. To this basic mixture you can then add various flavorings, such as vanilla, lemon, or chocolate.

basic cupcake recipe

1 stick (8 tablespoons) butter, at room temperature

½ cup granulated sugar

2 eggs

1 cup self-rising flour

2 tablespoons milk

1 teaspoon pure vanilla extract, grated zest of 1 lemon or 2 tablespoons cocoa powder (optional)

a 12-cup muffin pan

makes 12

Preheat the oven to 350°F, then line the muffin pan with paper liners.

Beat the butter and sugar together in a bowl until pale and fluffy. You can do this either by hand, or using an electric mixer. Then beat in the eggs, one at a time.

Sift over the flour, then fold in by hand. Stir in the milk and flavoring (if using) to make a creamy, spoonable mixture.

Spoon heaped tablespoonfuls of the mixture into each muffin cup, then bake for about 17 minutes until risen and golden and a skewer inserted into the center comes out clean.

Transfer the cupcakes to a wire rack and let cool completely before decorating.

decorating cupcakes

Most cakes can be made the day before and stored in an airtight container, but they're usually better decorated shortly before serving. There are literally hundreds of ways to decorate cupcakes, from a simple dusting of confectioners' sugar to thick swirls of creamy frosting. You can also add an array of decorations and toppings, from glacé cherries or toasted nuts to intricate sugar decorations available from large supermarkets and specialty kitchen shops.

First of all, you need to decide whether you want elegant flat-topped cupcakes or cheeky domed ones. Domed cupcakes are ideal for thick and creamy frostings, such as cream cheese frosting or chocolate ganache, or you can spoon over a glacé or fondant icing and let it spread over the top.

Flat-topped cupcakes are well suited to fondant and glacé icings that can be spooned on top and left to settle into a glossy, smooth surface. For flat-topped cupcakes, put a little less cake mixture in each muffin cup, then carefully slice off the domed tops using a serrated knife once baked and cooled.

fondant icing

For domed cupcakes, gradually beat 1½ cups sifted confectioners' sugar into 1 egg white, then beat in ¾ teaspoon lemon juice to make a thick, glossy icing. To color, stir in a couple of drops of food coloring at a time to achieve the desired color. Spoon onto the cupcakes, allowing the icing to spread down the domed top in drizzles.

For flat-topped cupcakes, beat 3 cups sifted confectioners' sugar into 2 egg whites, followed by 2½ teaspoons lemon juice to make a thick, glossy icing. To color, stir in a couple of drops of food coloring at a time to achieve the desired color. Spoon onto the cakes, allowing the icing to spread to the edges of the paper liner and settle in a glossy, smooth surface.

glacé icing

Put 1½ tablespoons lemon juice in a bowl, then gradually beat in 1¼ cups sifted confectioners' sugar to achieve a smooth, spoonable consistency. If necessary, add a drop more lemon juice or a little more icing sugar. To color, simply beat in a few drops of food coloring to achieve the desired color.

chocolate ganache

Put 4 oz. chopped bittersweet chocolate in a heatproof bowl. Heat ½ cup heavy cream in a saucepan until almost boiling, then pour it over the chocolate and let stand for 5 minutes. Stir the chocolate and cream together until smooth. Let cool for 30–60 minutes until thick and glossy, then spread over the cupcakes.

cream cheese frosting

Beat 6 oz. cream cheese, ⅓ cup confectioners' sugar, and 2 teaspoons lemon juice together until smooth and creamy. Swirl on top of the cupcakes.

simple cupcakes

A plateful of these pretty, passion fruit-scented cupcakes look like a swarm of fluttering butterflies. They remind me of the children's tea parties of my youth, where you were guaranteed to find a batch of butterfly cupcakes clustered on the tea table.

passion fruit butterfly cakes

3 passion fruit

1 stick (8 tablespoons) butter, at room temperature

½ cup granulated sugar

2 eggs

1 cup self-rising flour

1 teaspoon baking powder

to decorate

6 passion fruit

⅔ cup mascarpone

4 tablespoons confectioners' sugar, sifted, plus extra for dusting

a 12-cup muffin pan

makes 12

Preheat the oven to 350°F, then line the muffin pan with paper liners.

Halve the passion fruit. Scoop the flesh into a strainer set over a bowl. Press with the back of a teaspoon to extract the juice.

Beat the butter and sugar together in a bowl until pale and fluffy, then beat in the eggs, one at a time. Sift the flour and baking powder into the mixture and fold in, then stir in the passion fruit juice.

Spoon the mixture into the muffin cups, then bake for about 17 minutes until risen and golden and a skewer inserted in the center comes out clean. Transfer to a wire rack to cool.

To make the topping, halve the passion fruit and scoop the flesh into a strainer set over a bowl. Press with the back of a teaspoon to extract the juice, then add the mascarpone and confectioners' sugar to the bowl. Mix until smooth and creamy. Cover and chill for about 30 minutes to thicken up.

Slice the top off each cupcake, then cut each top in half. Spoon a dollop of the mascarpone mixture onto each cupcake, then top with the two halves, setting them at an angle to resemble wings. Dust with confectioners' sugar and serve.

Sweet with coconut and tangy with lime, these golden cupcakes with their snowy-white, ruffled tops look stunning arranged on a colored plate. Serve them mid-morning with coffee, mid-afternoon with tea, or after dinner as a simple dessert.

creamy coconut cupcakes

6 tablespoons butter, at room temperature

2 tablespoons coconut cream

½ cup granulated sugar

2 eggs

¼ cup self-rising flour

1 teaspoon baking powder

3 tablespoons dried coconut

grated zest of 1 lime

2 tablespoons milk

to decorate

5 oz. cream cheese

⅓ cup confectioners' sugar, sifted

2 teaspoons lime juice

coconut shavings

a 12-cup muffin pan

makes 12

Preheat the oven to 350°F, then line the muffin pan with paper liners.

Beat the butter, coconut cream, and sugar together in a bowl until pale and fluffy, then beat in the eggs, one at a time. Sift the flour and baking powder into the mixture and fold in. Stir in the dried coconut and lime zest, followed by the milk.

Spoon the mixture into the muffin cups, then bake for about 17 minutes until risen and golden and a skewer inserted in the center comes out clean. Transfer to a wire rack to cool.

To decorate, beat the cream cheese, confectioners' sugar, and lime juice together in a bowl. Swirl the frosting on top of the cupcakes, then sprinkle over the coconut shavings.

Warm, nutty and fragrant with orange zest, these light, fluffy, gluten- and dairy-free cupcakes are plain and simple without being in the least bit dull. They melt in the mouth and are perfect served while still warm from the oven. They're delicious simply dusted with confectioners' sugar, but for those who can't do without a little indulgence, serve them with a dollop of crème fraîche or cream on top.

orange and almond cupcakes

2 eggs

7 tablespoons granulated sugar

grated zest of 1 orange

¾ cup ground almonds

3 tablespoons potato flour

about ⅓ cup slivered almonds

confectioners' sugar, for dusting

a 12-cup muffin pan

makes 12

Preheat the oven to 325°F, then line the muffin pan with paper liners.

Put the eggs and sugar in a bowl and beat for 5–10 minutes until thick and pale. Add the orange zest, then sift the ground almonds and potato flour into the mixture and fold in.

Spoon the mixture into the muffin cups and sprinkle the slivered almonds over the top. Bake for about 22 minutes until risen and golden and a skewer inserted in the center comes out clean. Transfer to a wire rack and let cool slightly before dusting with confectioners' sugar and serving.

Maple syrup and pecans are a classic combination, and no better anywhere than in these light, sticky cupcakes topped with creamy, buttery frosting and caramelized pecans. Look out for the darker, amber maple syrup as it has a more intense flavor that really shines through in the fluffy, buttery cake.

maple and pecan cupcakes

1 stick (8 tablespoons) butter, at room temperature

¼ cup packed brown sugar

⅔ cup pure maple syrup

2 eggs

1 cup self-rising flour

½ cup pecan nuts, roughly chopped

to decorate

½ cup granulated sugar

12 pecan nut halves

3 tablespoons butter, at room temperature

3 tablespoons pure maple syrup

1¼ cups confectioners' sugar, sifted

a 12-cup muffin pan

makes 12

Preheat the oven to 350°F, then line the muffin pan with paper liners.

Beat the butter and sugar together in a bowl until creamy, then beat in the maple syrup. Beat in the eggs, one at a time, then sift the flour into the mixture and fold in. Fold in the nuts, then spoon the mixture into the muffin cups and bake for about 17 minutes until risen and golden and a skewer inserted in the center comes out clean. Transfer to a wire rack to cool.

To make the caramelized pecans, put the granulated sugar in a saucepan and add 2 tablespoons water. Heat gently, stirring, until the sugar melts and dissolves. Increase the heat and boil for about 6 minutes until it turns a pale gold color. Spread the nuts out on a sheet of parchment paper and spoon over a little of the caramel to cover each nut individually. Let cool.

Beat the butter, maple syrup, and confectioners' sugar together in a bowl until pale and fluffy. Spread the mixture over the cupcakes and top each one with a caramelized pecan.

These soft, sticky, dark brown cupcakes are dense and gingery, and delicious drizzled with a simple lemon icing. If you want elegant flat-topped cupcakes, make them in large liners, but if you prefer domed cupcakes with icing drizzling down the sides, make them in regular size liners.

gingerbread cupcakes with lemon icing

4 tablespoons butter

¼ cup packed brown sugar

2 tablespoons light corn syrup

2 tablespoons dark molasses

1 teaspoon ground ginger

⅓ cup milk

1 egg, beaten

2 pieces of stem ginger in syrup, drained and chopped

1 cup self-rising flour

to decorate

2 tablespoons lemon juice

1⅔ cups confectioners' sugar, sifted

2–3 pieces of stem ginger in syrup, drained and chopped

a 12-cup muffin pan

makes 12

Preheat the oven to 325°F, then line the muffin pan with paper liners.

Put the butter, sugar, corn syrup, molasses, and ground ginger in a saucepan and heat gently until melted. Remove the pan from the heat and stir in the milk, then beat in the egg and stem ginger.

Sift the flour into the mixture and fold in. Spoon the mixture into the muffin cups and bake for about 20 minutes until risen and a skewer inserted in the center comes out clean. Transfer to a wire rack to cool.

To decorate, pour the lemon juice into a bowl. Gradually sift in the confectioners' sugar, stirring, until smooth, thick, and spoonable. Spoon the icing over the cupcakes and put a few pieces of stem ginger on each one. Let set before serving.

½ cup packed brown sugar

⅔ cup sunflower oil

2 eggs

grated zest of 1 orange

seeds from 5 cardamom pods, crushed

½ teaspoon ground ginger

1½ cups self-rising flour

2 carrots, grated (about 1 cup grated carrot)

½ cup walnuts or pecan nuts, roughly chopped

to decorate

5 oz. mascarpone

finely grated zest of 1 orange

1½ teaspoons lemon juice

⅓ cup confectioners' sugar, sifted

a 12-cup muffin pan

makes 12

Lightly spiced and topped with a creamy citrus mascarpone frosting, these delightful little cupcakes are just the thing when you need a treat. They're not too sweet, but offer just the right combination of crunch, crumble, spice, sweetness, and creaminess—plus that little hint of naughtiness that a cupcake should always have.

carrot and cardamom cupcakes

Preheat the oven to 350°F, then line the muffin pan with paper liners.

Put the sugar in a bowl and break up using the back of a fork, then beat in the oil and eggs. Stir in the orange zest, crushed cardamom seeds, and ginger, then sift the flour into the mixture and fold in, followed by the carrots and nuts.

Spoon the mixture into the muffin cups and bake for about 20 minutes until risen and a skewer inserted in the center comes out clean. Transfer to a wire rack to cool.

To decorate, beat the mascarpone, orange zest, lemon juice, and confectioners' sugar together in a bowl and spread over the cupcakes.

Using yellow cornmeal gives these cupcakes a distinctive texture with an almost crispy bite and a gloriously rich color. Studded with juicy blueberries and topped with a rich, zesty cream cheese frosting, they offer the perfect pairing of light, fresh fruit and rich, creamy indulgence.

blueberry and lemon cupcakes

⅓ cup fine-ground yellow cornmeal

⅓ cup all-purpose flour

1 teaspoon baking powder

1 tablespoon crème fraîche or sour cream

1½ tablespoons sunflower oil

grated zest of 1 lemon

1 tablespoon lemon juice

1 egg

¼ cup granulated sugar

½ cup fresh blueberries

to decorate

5 oz. cream cheese

⅔ cup confectioners' sugar, sifted

½ teaspoon grated lemon zest

1 tablespoon lemon juice

about ½ cup fresh blueberries

strips of lemon zest

a muffin pan

makes 10

Preheat the oven to 350°F, then line the muffin pan with ten paper liners.

Combine the cornmeal, flour, and baking powder in a bowl, then set aside. Beat the crème fraîche, oil, and the lemon zest and juice together in a small pitcher, then set aside.

In a separate bowl, beat the egg and sugar together for about 4 minutes until thick and pale, then add the lemon mixture and fold in. Sift the cornmeal mixture over the top and fold in to combine.

Spoon the mixture into the muffin cups, then drop about 4 blueberries on top of each one, gently pressing them into the mixture. Bake for 15–16 minutes until risen and golden and a skewer inserted in the center comes out clean. Transfer to a wire rack to cool.

To decorate, beat the cream cheese in a bowl until creamy, then beat in the confectioner's sugar, lemon zest, and lemon juice. Swirl big dollops of frosting on top of the cupcakes and decorate with fresh blueberries and strips of lemon zest.

3½ oz. bittersweet chocolate

10 tablespoons butter,
at room temperature

¼ cup granulated sugar

2 eggs

2 tablespoons cocoa powder

¾ cup self-rising flour

2 teaspoons instant coffee,
dissolved in 1 tablespoon
boiling water

¼ cup chocolate-covered
coffee beans

to decorate

7 tablespoons butter,
at room temperature

1⅔ cups confectioners'
sugar, sifted

2 teaspoons instant coffee,
dissolved in 1 tablespoon
boiling water

grated bittersweet chocolate

a 12-cup muffin pan

makes 12

These rich, dark, chocolatey cupcakes studded with chocolate-covered coffee beans and topped with a creamy coffee butter frosting are simply divine. Dusted with grated chocolate, they look like a plateful of mini cappuccinos—but don't eat too many or they might keep you awake all night!

choca-mocha cupcakes

Preheat the oven to 350°F, then line the muffin pan with paper liners.

Melt the chocolate in a heatproof bowl set over a saucepan of simmering water or in a microwave, then set aside to cool.

Beat the butter and sugar together in a bowl until pale and fluffy, then beat in the eggs, one at a time. Stir in the melted chocolate and cocoa powder. Sift the flour into the mixture and stir in, then stir in the dissolved coffee, followed by the coffee beans.

Spoon the mixture into the muffin cups and bake for about 20 minutes until risen and a skewer inserted in the center comes out clean. Transfer to a wire rack to cool.

To decorate, beat the butter, confectioners' sugar, and dissolved coffee together in a bowl until pale and fluffy. Spread the mixture smoothly over the cupcakes and sprinkle with grated chocolate.

Subtly scented with lavender, these golden, buttery cupcakes are deliciously simple with an understated elegance, so they're perfect for serving mid-afternoon with a cup of tea. The fragrant taste of the lavender flowers gives the cupcakes an elusive hint that you can't quite put your finger on.

lavender cupcakes

½ cup granulated sugar

¼ teaspoon dried lavender flowers

1 stick (8 tablespoons) butter, at room temperature

2 eggs

1 cup self-rising flour

2 tablespoons milk

to decorate

1½ cups confectioners' sugar, sifted

1 egg white

lilac food coloring

12 sprigs of fresh lavender

a 12-cup muffin pan

makes 12

Preheat the oven to 350°F, then line the muffin pan with paper liners.

Put the sugar and lavender flowers in a food processor and process briefly to combine. Tip the lavender sugar into a bowl with the butter and beat together until pale and fluffy.

Beat the eggs into the butter mixture, one at a time, then sift in the flour and fold in. Stir in the milk, then spoon the mixture into the muffin cups. Bake for about 18 minutes until risen and golden and a skewer inserted in the center comes out clean, then transfer to a wire rack to cool.

To decorate, gradually beat the confectioners' sugar into the egg white in a bowl, then add a few drops of food coloring and stir to achieve a lavender-colored icing. Spoon the icing over the cupcakes, then top each one with a sprig of fresh lavender. Let set before serving.

Delicately scented with rosewater, these gorgeous pink cupcakes are perfect for girls who like things extra-pretty. I prefer pale pink sugared rose petals on mine, but darker pink or white will look just as lovely.

rosewater cupcakes

1 stick (8 tablespoons) butter, at room temperature

½ cup granulated sugar

2 eggs

1 cup self-rising flour

1 tablespoon rosewater

to decorate

12 pink rose petals

1 egg white, beaten

1 tablespoon superfine sugar

1½–2 tablespoons lemon juice

1¼ cups confectioners' sugar

pink food coloring

a 12-cup muffin pan

makes 12

Preheat the oven to 350°F, then line the muffin pan with paper liners.

Beat the butter and sugar together in a bowl until pale and fluffy, then beat in the eggs, one at a time. Sift the flour into the mixture and fold in, then stir in the rosewater.

Spoon the mixture into the muffin cups and bake for about 17 minutes until risen and golden and a skewer inserted in the center comes out clean. Transfer to a wire rack to cool.

To decorate, brush each rose petal with egg white, then sprinkle with superfine sugar and let dry for about 1 hour.

Put 1½ tablespoons lemon juice in a bowl, then sift the confectioners' sugar into the bowl and stir until smooth. Add a little more lemon juice as required to make a smooth, spoonable icing. Add one or two drops of food coloring to achieve a pale pink frosting, then drizzle over the cupcakes. Top each one with a sugared rose petal. Let set before serving.

With a subtle pale green to the crumb and a subtle taste of pistachio, these little cupcakes are utterly irresistible and unbelievably girly. (Which is just the way they should be!) To achieve a pale pistachio-colored icing, use a pale green food coloring if you can find one, adding a little at a time until you achieve just the right shade.

pistachio cupcakes

⅓ cup pistachio nuts

1 stick (8 tablespoons) butter, at room temperature

½ cup granulated sugar

2 eggs

¾ cup self-rising flour

2 tablespoons milk

to decorate

1 egg white

1½ cups confectioners' sugar

¼ teaspoon lemon juice

green food coloring

12 pink rice paper roses

a 12-cup muffin pan

makes 12

Preheat the oven to 350°F, then line the muffin pan with paper liners.

Put the pistachio nuts in a food processor and process until finely ground. Set aside.

Beat the butter and sugar together in a bowl until pale and fluffy, then beat in the eggs, one at a time. Stir in the ground nuts, then sift the flour into the mixture and fold in. Stir in the milk and spoon the mixture into the muffin cups. Bake for about 18 minutes until risen and golden and a skewer inserted in the center comes out clean. Transfer to a wire rack to cool.

To decorate, put the egg white in a bowl and gradually sift over the confectioners' sugar, beating in as you go until thick and glossy, then beat in the lemon juice. The icing should be thick but spoonable.

Add a few drops of food coloring to the icing and beat to make a pale pistachio green icing. Spoon on top of the cupcakes and top each one with a pink rice paper rose. Let set before serving.

celebration cupcakes

Bake a batch of these delightfully flirtatious cupcakes filled with a zesty lemon cream and fresh raspberries for the one you love, and they'll never have eyes for anyone but you! For that extra special touch, buy a muffin pan with heart-shaped cups and push your regular paper liners into the cups.

raspberry love-heart cupcakes

1 stick (8 tablespoons) butter, at room temperature

½ cup granulated sugar

2 eggs

1 cup self-rising flour

grated zest and juice of ½ lemon

to decorate

⅓ cup crème fraîche or sour cream

1 tablespoon jarred lemon curd

⅔ cup fresh raspberries

confectioners' sugar, for dusting

a 12-cup muffin pan

makes 12

Preheat the oven to 350°F, then line the muffin pan with paper liners.

Beat the butter and sugar together in a bowl until pale and fluffy, then beat in the eggs, one at a time. Sift the flour into the mixture and fold in, then stir in the lemon zest and juice. Spoon the mixture into the muffin cups and bake for about 18 minutes until risen and golden and a skewer inserted in the center comes out clean. Transfer to a wire rack to cool.

To decorate, using a sharp, pointed knife, remove a deep round from the center of each cake, about 1¼ inches in diameter. Slice the pointed bit off each piece of cored-out cake so that you are left with a flat round. Using a mini heart-shaped cutter, cut the rounds into heart shapes.

Combine the crème fraîche and lemon curd in a bowl, then fold in the raspberries. Spoon the mixture into the hollowed-out cupcakes, then top with the hearts. Dust with confectioners' sugar.

4 tablespoons butter,
at room temperature

⅓ cup packed brown sugar

1 egg

grated zest of 1 orange

½ cup self-rising flour

1 tablespoon brandy

4 dried figs, chopped

3 tablespoons golden raisins

½ cup glacé cherries, halved

to decorate

3½ oz. blue ready-to-roll
fondant icing

3 cups confectioners'
sugar, sifted

3 egg whites

2½ teaspoons lemon juice

edible silver balls

edible sparkles

pale blue or silver ribbon
(optional)

a mini star-shaped cookie cutter

a 12-cup muffin pan

makes 12

These pretty pale blue and silver cupcakes are just the thing to get you in the festive mood. The fragrant, fruity buns are much lighter than traditional English Christmas cake. Remember to make the fondant stars the day before to give them time to firm up. If you can't find any blue fondant icing, simply add a few drops of blue food coloring to white fondant icing and knead to make a pale blue icing.

christmas cupcakes

Make the star decorations the day before you plan to make the cupcakes. Roll out the fondant icing, then use the cookie cutter to cut out 12 stars. Set aside and let dry overnight.

To make the cupcakes, preheat the oven to 350°F, then line the muffin pan with paper liners.

Beat the butter and sugar together in a bowl until creamy. Beat in the egg, a little at a time, then stir in the orange zest. Sift the flour into the mixture and fold in, then stir in the brandy, followed by the dried fruit and glacé cherries.

Spoon the mixture into the muffin cups and bake for about 14 minutes until risen and golden and a skewer inserted in the center comes out clean. Transfer to a wire rack to cool.

To decorate, carefully tie a piece of ribbon in a bow around each cupcake, if liked. Gradually beat the confectioners' sugar into two of the egg whites in a bowl until smooth and creamy, then beat in the lemon juice. Spoon the mixture over the cupcakes and scatter over the silver balls. Let the icing firm up slightly.

Place the star decorations on top of the cupcakes, brush with the remaining beaten egg white, and scatter with sparkles.

Who wants an old-fashioned tiered wedding cake when you could have a mountain of these pretty white wedding cupcakes instead? I like the full-on white look when it comes to the decorations, but you can add pastel food coloring, flowers, or ribbon according to your color scheme. You can also use different size muffin pans to make a variety of sizes.

wedding cupcakes

1 stick (8 tablespoons) butter, at room temperature

½ cup granulated sugar

2 eggs

1 cup self-rising flour

1 teaspoon pure vanilla extract or grated lemon zest

2 tablespoons milk

to decorate

1 egg white

1 cup confectioners' sugar, sifted

½ teaspoon lemon juice

white edible flower decorations

white lace or organza ribbon

a 12-cup muffin pan

makes 12

Preheat the oven to 350°F, then line the muffin pan with paper liners.

Beat the butter and sugar together in a bowl until pale and fluffy, then beat in the eggs, one at a time. Sift the flour into the mixture and fold in, then stir in the vanilla extract or lemon zest and the milk.

Spoon the mixture into the muffin cups and bake for about 18 minutes until risen and golden and a skewer inserted in the center comes out clean. Transfer to a wire rack to cool.

To decorate, carefully tie a piece of ribbon around each cupcake. Put the egg white in a large bowl, then beat in the confectioners' sugar until thick and creamy. Beat in the lemon juice to make a thick, spoonable icing. (If necessary, add a drizzle more lemon juice or a little more sugar to get the right consistency.)

Spoon the icing onto the cupcakes, then top each one with a flower. The icing hardens quite fast, so work quickly as soon as you've made the icing.

Sweet, spicy pumpkin cupcakes topped with pretty white and dark chocolate cobwebs are definitely a treat rather than a trick. You can leave the topping to set completely if you like, but they're so much better when the chocolate topping is still soft.

halloween cupcakes

½ cup packed brown sugar

½ cup sunflower oil

2 eggs

1 cup grated butternut squash or pumpkin

grated zest of 1 lemon

1 cup self-rising flour

1 teaspoon baking powder

1 teaspoon ground cinnamon

to decorate

5 oz. white chocolate, chopped

1 oz. bittersweet chocolate

a 12-cup muffin pan

makes 12

Preheat the oven to 350°F, then line the muffin pan with paper liners.

Put the sugar in a bowl and break up with the back of a fork, then beat in the oil and eggs. Fold in the grated squash or pumpkin and lemon zest. Combine the flour, baking powder, and cinnamon in a bowl, then sift into the cake mixture and fold in.

Spoon the mixture into the muffin cups and bake for about 18 minutes until risen and a skewer inserted in the center comes out clean. Transfer to a wire rack to cool.

To decorate, put the white and bittersweet chocolate in two separate heatproof bowls. Melt over a saucepan of simmering water or in a microwave. Let cool slightly, then spoon the white chocolate over the cupcakes.

Cut a large square of parchment paper and fold into eighths to make a cone and tape together. Spoon the bittersweet chocolate into the cone and snip the tip off so that you can pipe a thin line of chocolate. Put a dot of chocolate in the center of each cake, then pipe three concentric circles around the dot.

Using a skewer, draw a line from the central dot to the outside edge of the cake and repeat about eight times all the way round to create a spider's web pattern. Serve while the chocolate is still slightly soft and gooey.

You'll never want a traditional birthday cake again after sampling these gooey, chocolatey and nutty baby brownie cupcakes. Pile them up on a cake stand or plate and gently press a candle into each one. Turn out the lights, light the candles, and voilà!

chocolate brownie birthday cupcakes

3½ oz. bittersweet chocolate, chopped

5 tablespoons butter

1 egg

⅓ cup granulated sugar

3 tablespoons self-rising flour

⅓ cup macadamia nuts, pecan nuts, or walnuts, coarsely chopped

twelve mini candles

two mini muffin pans

makes 18

Preheat the oven to 350°F, then line the mini muffin pans with 18 mini muffin or petit fours liners.

Put the chocolate and butter in a heatproof bowl set over a saucepan of gently simmering water and heat, stirring until melted. Remove from the heat and set aside to cool slightly.

When the mixture has cooled, beat in the egg, then stir in the sugar. Sift the flour into the mixture and fold in, then stir in the nuts. Spoon the mixture into the muffin cups and bake for about 17 minutes until the top has turned pale and crackly and is just firm to the touch. Transfer to a wire rack to cool, before serving with a glowing candle in the center of each one.

These pretty floral cupcakes are perfect for welcoming in the beginning of spring, the warmer weather, and the arrival of spring flowers. You could also offer them as a gift for Mother's Day or Easter. Although you can find plenty of simple sugar flower decorations in most supermarkets, it's worth searching out specialty kitchen shops with a wider selection of more unusual and interesting flowers.

spring flower cupcakes

1 stick (8 tablespoons) butter, at room temperature

½ cup granulated sugar

2 eggs

1 cup self-rising flour

1 teaspoon pure vanilla extract

2 tablespoons milk

to decorate

2 egg whites

2 cups confectioners' sugar, sifted

2½ teaspoons lemon juice

green and yellow food coloring

12 sugar spring flowers, such as daffodils or daisies

a 12-cup muffin pan

makes 12

Preheat the oven to 350°F, then line the muffin pan with paper liners.

Beat the butter and sugar together in a bowl until pale and fluffy, then beat in the eggs, one at a time. Sift the flour into the mixture and fold in, then stir in the vanilla extract and milk. Spoon the mixture into the muffin cups and bake for about 15 minutes until risen and golden and a skewer inserted in the center comes out clean. Transfer to a wire rack to cool.

If any of the cupcakes have domed above the level of the paper liner, gently slice off the top using a serrated knife to create a flat surface.

To decorate, put the egg whites in a bowl and gradually beat in the confectioners' sugar, then the lemon juice to give a thick, glossy, spoonable icing.

Divide the icing between two bowls and tint one with green food coloring and the other with yellow to create pretty, fresh pastel shades. Spoon the icing over the cupcakes—it should naturally spread to the edges of the paper liners. If any air bubbles appear, gently prick with a toothpick, then top each cupcake with a sugar flower. The icing will firm up and set within 1 hour.

For their sheer cuteness alone, these pastel-colored mini cupcakes are absolutely irresistible. Bake up a batch as a gift for a new mother to celebrate the arrival of her newborn. The white chocolate topping sets, so they're ideal for packing up in a pretty gift box—and just the treat she'll need to get her through those first few sleepless nights.

vanilla and white chocolate babycakes

4 tablespoons butter, at room temperature

5 tablespoons granulated sugar

1 egg, beaten

½ cup self-rising flour

¼ teaspoon pure vanilla extract

1 tablespoon milk

to decorate

2 oz. white chocolate, chopped

green food coloring

pink food coloring

15 brightly colored candies

a 12-cup mini muffin pan or a baking sheet

makes 12

Preheat the oven to 350°F, then line the muffin pan with petit fours liners. (If you don't have a mini muffin pan, arrange the liners on a baking sheet; the liners should be able to cope with such a small amount of mixture.)

Beat the butter and sugar together in a bowl until pale and fluffy, then beat in the egg, a little at a time. Sift the flour into the mixture and fold in, then stir in the vanilla extract and milk.

Spoon the mixture into the muffin cups, then bake for about 15 minutes until risen and golden and the tops spring back when gently pressed. Transfer to a wire rack to cool.

To decorate, divide the chocolate among three heatproof bowls and melt over a saucepan of simmering water or in a microwave. Let cool slightly, then stir a couple of drops of green food coloring into one bowl of chocolate and a couple of drops of pink into another. Leave the third bowl of chocolate plain.

Spoon white chocolate over four of the cupcakes, pink over another four, and green over the remaining four, then top each one with a candy. Serve while the chocolate is still soft, or let set and package up as a gift.

Whether it's the 4th of July or Bastille Day, these sparkling celebration cupcakes are just the thing to serve when the night sky is exploding with brightly colored stars. Take a plate of these dense, moist, citrusy chocolate cupcakes topped with sparklers outside while you watch the fireworks.

firework cupcakes

1 cup all-purpose flour

3 tablespoons cocoa powder

½ teaspoon baking soda

¼ cup granulated sugar

½ cup orange juice

grated zest of 1 orange

3 tablespoons sunflower oil

1½ teaspoons distilled white vinegar

to decorate

3½ oz. bittersweet chocolate, chopped

½ cup heavy cream

tiny edible silver balls or stars

12 mini sparklers

a 12-cup muffin pan

makes 12

Preheat the oven to 350°F, then line the muffin pan with paper liners.

Combine the flour, cocoa, baking soda, and sugar in a bowl. Sift into a larger bowl and make a well in the center.

Combine the orange juice and zest, oil and vinegar in pitcher and pour into the dry ingredients. Quickly stir together until combined, then spoon the mixture into the muffin cups. (It should be quite liquid and gooey, so you may find a small ladle useful.)

Bake for about 15 minutes until risen and firm on top and a skewer inserted in the center comes out clean. Transfer to a wire rack to cool.

To decorate, put the chocolate in a heatproof bowl. Heat the cream in a saucepan until almost boiling, then pour over the chocolate. Let stand for about 5 minutes, then stir until smooth and creamy. Let cool for 5–10 minutes more until thick and glossy, then spread over the cupcakes.

Sprinkle the frosted cupcakes with tiny silver balls or stars and stick a sparkler in the center of each one. Light the sparklers before serving.

indulgent cupcakes

Topped with a cool, creamy mascarpone topping and golden shards of praline, these little cupcakes offer a pure taste of heaven. A hint of bitter coffee brings out and enhances the flavor of the nutty praline.

coffee and praline cupcakes

½ cup sugar

scant ½ cup blanched hazelnuts

1 stick (8 tablespoons) butter, at room temperature

2 eggs

⅔ cup self-rising flour

1 teaspoon baking powder

2 teaspoons instant coffee, dissolved in 1 tablespoon boiling water

to decorate

2 tablespoons granulated sugar

¼ cup blanched hazelnuts, roughly chopped

scant ½ cup mascarpone

⅔ cup confectioners' sugar, sifted

1 teaspoon instant coffee, dissolved in ½ tablespoon boiling water

a 12-cup muffin pan

a baking sheet

makes 12

Preheat the oven to 350°F. Line the muffin pan with paper liners and the baking sheet with parchment paper.

Put half the sugar in a dry pan and heat gently, stirring, for about 5 minutes until melted and pale gold. Add the hazelnuts and cook, stirring, for about 1 minute, then pour onto the lined baking sheet and let harden for at least 20 minutes.

Break the hardened praline into pieces and place in a food processor, then process until finely ground. Set aside.

Beat the butter and the remaining sugar together in a bowl until pale and fluffy, then beat in the ground praline. Beat in the eggs, one at a time, then sift the flour and baking powder into the mixture and fold in. Stir in the dissolved coffee, then spoon the mixture into the muffin cups and bake for about 16 minutes until risen and golden and a skewer inserted in the center comes out clean. Transfer to a wire rack to cool.

To decorate, put the sugar in a dry pan and heat gently, stirring, for about 5 minutes until melted and pale gold. Add the hazelnuts and cook, stirring, for about 30 seconds, then pour onto the lined baking sheet. Let harden for about 20 minutes, then break into small shards.

Beat the mascarpone and confectioners' sugar in a bowl until smooth, then stir in the dissolved coffee. Swirl the mixture onto the cupcakes and decorate with shards of praline.

With a gooey chocolate and hazelnut center, these luscious cupcakes are deliciously tender. Stirring chocolate and hazelnut spread into the frosting gives it a wonderfully nutty taste to complement the toasted hazelnuts on top.

gooey chocolate and hazelnut cupcakes

2½ oz. bittersweet chocolate, chopped

6½ tablespoons butter, at room temperature

½ cup granulated sugar

2 eggs

3 tablespoons blanched hazelnuts, ground

¾ cup self-rising flour

½ cup chocolate and hazelnut spread, such as Nutella

to decorate

3½ oz. bittersweet chocolate, chopped

⅓ cup heavy cream

2 tablespoons chocolate and hazelnut spread, such as Nutella

about 3 tablespoons blanched hazelnuts, toasted and cut into large pieces

a 12-cup muffin pan

makes 12

Preheat the oven to 350°F, then line the muffin pan with paper liners.

Melt the chocolate in a heatproof bowl set over a saucepan of simmering water or in the microwave, then set aside to cool.

Beat the butter and sugar together in a bowl until pale and fluffy, then beat in the eggs, one at a time. Stir in the ground hazelnuts, then sift the flour into the mixture and fold in. Stir in the melted chocolate.

Drop ½ heaped tablespoonful of the mixture into each muffin cup, then flatten and make an indentation in the center of each dollop of mixture using the back of a teaspoon. Drop a generous dollop of chocolate spread into the center of each one, then top with the remaining cake mixture. Bake for about 18 minutes until risen and the tops spring back when gently pressed. Transfer to a wire rack to cool.

To decorate, put the chocolate in a heatproof bowl. Heat the cream in a saucepan until almost boiling, then pour over the chocolate and let stand for 5 minutes. Stir until smooth and creamy, then stir in the chocolate spread. Let cool for about 30 minutes until thick and glossy.

Spread the frosting over the cupcakes and arrange a cluster of nuts in the center of each one.

Inspired by the English classic banoffee pie, these creamy cupcakes are simply to die for. The tender, moist banana cupcakes are packed with nuggets of chewy caramel, then topped with whipped cream, sweet dulce de leche, and fresh banana. If you can't find the Spanish dulce de leche, make your own following the instructions below.

banoffee cupcakes

4 tablespoons butter, at room temperature

⅓ cup packed brown sugar

1 egg

1 ripe banana, mashed

1 cup self-rising flour

4 chewy caramels, chopped

to decorate

⅔ cup heavy cream, whipped

3–4 tablespoons dulce de leche

1 banana, sliced

a muffin pan

makes 10

Preheat the oven to 350°F, then line the muffin pan with ten paper liners.

Beat the butter and sugar together in a bowl until creamy, then beat in the egg, a little at a time. Fold in the mashed banana, then sift the flour into the mixture and fold in, followed by the caramels.

Spoon the mixture into the muffin cups and bake for about 16 minutes until risen and a skewer inserted in the center comes out clean. Transfer to a wire rack to cool.

To decorate, swirl the cream over each of the cupcakes, then drizzle with a spoonful of dulce de leche and top with slices of banana.

Note Dulce de leche is a sweet, thick caramel sauce from Spain, that is available from larger supermarkets. If you can't find it, you can make it yourself. Put a sealed can of sweetened condensed milk in a saucepan, pour over boiling water to cover and boil for three hours, adding more water as necessary so that the can is always covered. Remove from the pan and let cool completely before opening using a can opener. Stir well to make a smooth sauce before spooning over the cupcakes.

These cupcakes, made using a classic genoise sponge, are light and creamy and perfect for serving in summer when fresh soft berries are sweet, juicy, and in season. Because the batter contains no fat, the cupcakes don't keep well, so are best eaten on the day they're made.

fresh fruit cupcakes

2 eggs

5 tablespoons granulated sugar

1 teaspoon pure vanilla extract

¼ cup all-purpose flour

to decorate

⅔ cup heavy cream

1 pint fresh summer berries, such as strawberries, blueberries, raspberries, and red currants

confectioners' sugar, for dusting

a 12-cup muffin pan

makes 12

Preheat the oven to 350°F, then line the muffin pan with paper liners.

Put the eggs and sugar in a large bowl and beat for about 10 minutes until thick and pale. Add the vanilla extract. Sift the flour into a separate bowl twice, then sift into the egg mixture and fold in.

Spoon the mixture into the muffin cups and bake for about 12 minutes until risen and golden and a skewer inserted in the center comes out clean. Transfer to a wire rack to cool.

To decorate, whip the cream in a bowl until it stands in peaks, then swirl over the cupcakes. Top with fresh berries, dust with confectioners' sugar, and serve immediately.

Vanilla-rich yellow cake topped with a thick layer of creamy vanilla and white chocolate cheesecake and decorated with fresh strawberries is the ultimate treat. These cupcakes are best chilled so that the creamy topping sets—but if you just can't wait, they're equally good while it's still soft. Top each cake with one big, fat, glistening strawberry, or nestle a few halves or tiny ones on top.

strawberry cheesecake cupcakes

4 tablespoons butter, at room temperature

5 tablespoons sugar

2 eggs

½ cup self-rising flour

½ teaspoon pure vanilla extract

2 tablespoons milk

to decorate

3 oz. white chocolate, chopped

3 oz. cream cheese

6 tablespoons crème fraîche or sour cream

1½ teaspoons pure vanilla extract

6 tablespoons confectioners' sugar, sifted

fresh strawberries

a 12-cup muffin pan

makes 12

Preheat the oven to 350°F, then line the muffin pan with paper liners.

Beat the butter and sugar together in a bowl until pale and fluffy, then beat in the egg, a little at a time. Sift the flour into the mixture and fold in, then stir in the vanilla extract and milk. Spoon the mixture into the muffin cups. Bake for about 10 minutes until risen and golden and a skewer inserted in the center comes out clean. Transfer to a wire rack to cool.

To decorate, check that none of the cupcakes have risen above the rim of the paper liners. If any have, carefully slice off the top using a serrated knife to create a flat surface.

Melt the chocolate in a heatproof bowl set over a saucepan of simmering water or in a microwave, then set aside to cool slightly. Beat the cream cheese, crème fraîche, vanilla extract, and confectioners' sugar together in a separate bowl, then beat in the melted chocolate.

Smooth the cream cheese mixture over the cupcakes, up to the rim of the paper liners, then chill for at least 1½ hours until set. Decorate with fresh strawberries and serve.

The combination of chocolate, marshmallows, and nuts in these sweet and sticky cupcakes is a taste of pure indulgence. If you've got a really sweet tooth, sprinkle a few extra mini marshmallows on top along with the nuts and chocolate chips, or if you prefer a more adult version, leave them spread simply with the chocolate topping.

rocky road cupcakes

1 stick (8 tablespoons) butter, at room temperature

½ cup granulated sugar

2 eggs

1 cup self-rising flour

3 tablespoons cocoa powder

3 tablespoons milk

1 oz. white chocolate chips

1 cup mini marshmallows

2 tablespoons slivered almonds or brazil nuts

to decorate

3½ oz. bittersweet chocolate, chopped

½ cup heavy cream

3 tablespoons slivered almonds or brazil nuts

¼ cup white chocolate chips

mini marshmallows (optional)

a 12-cup muffin pan

makes 12

Preheat the oven to 350°F, then line the muffin pan with paper liners.

Beat the butter and sugar together in a bowl until pale and fluffy, then beat in the eggs, one at a time. Sift the flour and cocoa into the mixture and fold in. Stir in the milk, followed by the chocolate chips, marshmallows, and nuts.

Spoon the mixture into the muffin cups and bake for about 18 minutes until risen and the tops spring back when lightly pressed. Transfer to a wire rack to cool.

Put the chocolate in a heatproof bowl. Heat the cream in a saucepan until almost boiling, then pour over the chocolate and let stand for 5 minutes. Stir until smooth and creamy, then let cool for about 30 minutes until thick and glossy.

Spread the chocolate mixture over the cupcakes and sprinkle with nuts, chocolate chips, and marshmallows, if liked.

Sinking your teeth into these golden, buttery cupcakes with their gooey lemon center and sticky white Italian meringue frosting is a sheer taste of heaven. Try to find a really good-quality jarred lemon curd for the filling to give these little cupcakes their really intense, lemony flavor.

lemon meringue cupcakes

1 stick (8 tablespoons) butter, at room temperature

½ cup granulated sugar

2 eggs

1 cup self-rising flour

grated zest and juice of 1 lemon

3 tablespoons jarred lemon curd

to decorate

¼ cup granulated sugar

2 egg whites

a 12-cup muffin pan

a piping bag fitted with a star tip (optional)

makes 12

Preheat the oven to 350°F, then line the muffin pan with paper liners.

Beat the butter and sugar together in a bowl until pale and fluffy, then beat in the eggs, one at a time. Sift the flour into the mixture and fold in, then stir in the lemon zest and juice.

Spoon a good dollop of the mixture into each muffin cup and make an indentation in the center with the back of a teaspoon. Drop in a dollop of lemon curd, then top with the remaining cake mixture.

Bake for about 17 minutes until risen and golden and a skewer inserted in the center comes out clean. Transfer to a wire rack to cool.

To decorate, put the sugar and egg whites in a bowl and set over a saucepan of simmering water. Beat constantly for about 5 minutes until the mixture is thick and glossy and stands in peaks. Use a piping bag with a star tip to pipe a whirl onto the top of each cake or swirl the meringue over the cupcakes using a spoon. The frosting will firm up as the cupcakes sit, so for a soft meringue, let set for at least 30 minutes, and for a firm meringue, let set for at least 3 hours.

Inspired by the classic Black Forest gateau, these dinky, crumbly chocolate cupcakes are studded with sweet, sticky cherries and spiked with kirsch. If you really want to go overboard on indulgence, serve them topped with a dollop of whipped cream as well, and shave over some dark chocolate curls.

black forest cupcakes

3 oz. bittersweet chocolate, chopped

1 stick (8 tablespoons) butter, at room temperature

½ cup sugar

2 eggs

2 tablespoons ground almonds

1¼ cups self-rising flour

1 tablespoon cocoa powder

2 tablespoons kirsch

½ cup glacé cherries, halved

to decorate

3½ oz. bittersweet chocolate, chopped

½ cup heavy cream

1 tablespoon kirsch

12 glacé cherries

a 12-cup muffin pan

makes 12

Preheat the oven to 350°F, then line the muffin pan with paper liners.

Melt the chocolate in a heatproof bowl set over a saucepan of simmering water or in a microwave, then set aside to cool.

Beat the butter and sugar together in a bowl until pale and fluffy, then beat in the eggs, one at a time. Beat in the melted chocolate, then stir in the almonds. Sift the flour and cocoa into the mixture and fold in, then fold in the kirsch, followed by the glacé cherries.

Spoon the mixture into the muffin cups and bake for about 20 minutes until a skewer inserted in the center comes out clean. Transfer to a wire rack to cool.

To decorate, put the chocolate in a heatproof bowl. Heat the cream in a saucepan until almost boiling, then pour over the chocolate and let stand for 5 minutes. Stir until smooth and creamy, then stir in the kirsch and let cool for about 1 hour until thick and glossy. Spread the frosting over the cupcakes and top with a glacé cherry.

index

conversion chart

Weights and measures have been rounded up
or down slightly to make measuring easier.

Measuring butter:

A US stick of butter weighs 4 oz. which is
approximately 115 g or 8 tablespoons. The recipes in
this book require the following conversions:

American	Metric	Imperial
6 tbsp	85 g	3 oz.
7 tbsp	100 g	3½ oz.
1 stick	115 g	4 oz.

Volume equivalents:

American	Metric	Imperial
1 teaspoon	5 ml	
1 tablespoon	15 ml	
¼ cup	60 ml	2 fl.oz.
⅓ cup	75 ml	2½ fl.oz.
½ cup	125 ml	4 fl.oz.
⅔ cup	150 ml	5 fl.oz. (¼ pint)
¾ cup	175 ml	6 fl.oz.
1 cup	250 ml	8 fl.oz.

Weight equivalents:

Imperial	Metric
1 oz.	30 g
2 oz.	55 g
3 oz.	85 g
3½ oz.	100 g
4 oz.	115 g
5 oz.	140 g
6 oz.	175 g
8 oz. (½ lb.)	225 g
9 oz.	250 g
10 oz.	280 g
11½ oz.	325 g
12 oz.	350 g
13 oz.	375 g
14 oz.	400 g
15 oz.	425 g
16 oz. (1 lb.)	450 g

Measurements:

Inches	cm
¼ inch	5 mm
½ inch	1 cm
¾ inch	1.5 cm
1 inch	2.5 cm
2 inches	5 cm
3 inches	7 cm
4 inches	10 cm
5 inches	12 cm
6 inches	15 cm
7 inches	18 cm
8 inches	20 cm
9 inches	23 cm
10 inches	25 cm
11 inches	28 cm
12 inches	30 cm

Oven temperatures:

150°C	(300°F)	Gas 2
170°C	(325°F)	Gas 3
180°C	(350°F)	Gas 4
190°C	(375°F)	Gas 5
200°C	(400°F)	Gas 6